PLAYER-COACH LEADER

LEVERAGE

THE TALENT AROUND YOU

LAMAR HAMILTON

TIGER OAK PUBLICATIONS

Minneapolis, MN

COPYRIGHT © 2007 BY LAMAR HAMILTON

Lamar Hamilton
P.O. Box 385816
Minneapolis, MN 55438

Email: lamar@lamarhamilton.com
Phone: 952-829-0651
www.playercoachleader.com

Player-Coach Leader[SM]: Leverage The Talent Around You
by Lamar Hamilton
ISBN: 978-0-9799280-0-0

Printed in the United States of America
First printing: October, 2007

Tiger Oak Publications, Inc.
Minneapolis, MN
Art Director | Marie Walter

THIS BOOK IS DEDICATED TO:
MONTY SHOLUND
1920-2007

Master sculptor of people into His image.

ith a heart of gratitude, I dedicate this book to the man who believed in me, affirmed me, challenged me to think big and said to me, "There is a book in you, Lamar. You must get to writing." The following email from Monty (one of several I saved and will keep forever) gave me the courage and determination to write this book. In his own words:

> *"You write so lucidly and powerfully, Lamar, and I am sure that Paul would have been impacted by both your candid advice and your balancing an individual's problem with corporate health and success. The whole article is so compelling and I enjoyed sharing it. Your insight into a complicated situation is what business executives need and I'm stimulated to share your procedure."*

As I wrote this book my goal was to live up to the challenge Monty put before me:

> *"The important thing is to be gripped by a passion for producing the volume, for the good of mankind and the Glory of God."*

Success must be measured by this standard. My hope is that both will be so.

If you had the privilege of experiencing Monty's scrutiny and admonition, you will see his influence in these pages. He is esteemed by a multitude of men and women around the globe. More importantly, Monty is in the presence of his Lord, whom he loved dearly and devoted all the days of his life to serving.

"Cheerio" to you, Monty!

INTRODUCTION

"If it weren't for the people issues, I could get a lot more done."

This is a phrase we've all heard, or maybe even said, in times of frustration.

Business is people. People exchanging services and products. People communicating expectations and assuming responsibility. People generating ideas and turning them into profitable enterprises. People buying and selling. People making things and marketing things. People building relationships and delivering on promises. People competing and collaborating. Business doesn't happen without people engaging with one another.

Yet new leaders and managers seem surprised when they encounter so many "people issues." But people *are* the issue. Your business depends on your ability to build and leverage the talent around you.

When I suggest coaching and developing people to leaders, I usually get the objection: "With the demands made on me, I just do not have time to develop people." I used to buy into that line – even admire the implied importance of those who said it—and empathize with the over-worked executive. But I have come to believe that, in most cases, this objection is a cover-up for either a low interest in people or a lack of ability to develop others.

In my work with these leaders, I have most often observed this attitude among the most competent and successful. It surfaces when their intense drive for results, love of competition and determination to break all previous records is restricted by incompetence and low commitment from others. The problem usually arises when the leaders have put people in key positions without verifying their readiness, and then handed out assignments based on the assumption that everyone knows what to do. The inevitable outcome is exasperation and the pronouncement that today's talent just isn't as committed as the previous generation was.

The people component is even more critical for service industry professionals, who depend on highly skilled talent to deliver the best solutions for their clients. The problem is twofold: First, there is a "war for talent" among professional services firms throughout the country; the specialized talent coming out of colleges does not match the business demand in some fields. Second, partners often encounter a shift in their firm's expectations as their career advances. They must manage a significant book of business, but they are also expected to delegate an increasing amount of their work to staff members. For professionals who have built their career on personal performance and effort, this can be a challenging transition to make. Many are just not interested; those who are often struggle with finding the right balance between doing and delegating the work.

So the question comes down to how busy executives, partners, directors and managers can build strong talent around them while meeting the demands of business. The answer lies in acquiring Player-Coach proficiencies that enable leaders to develop people through their work, in the course of the regular business day.

With you as a Player-Coach Leader^{SM}, members of your team will reveal abilities you never would have discovered otherwise. They will be ready any time to execute the play you call, even in a crucial last-second play when the game is on the line. And as time passes, the successful team you build will be a shining part of your legacy.

This book was written to show how it's not only possible, but imperative — and even enjoyable — to acquire these skills. It tells a story of a high-performing leader who struggles to maintain his impressive business productivity while learning to place a higher priority on his team. He comes face to face with his limitations in the midst of great success and learns, from someone he respects, how to embrace something he never really cared about – developing other people.

In writing this book, I have created characters, companies and events similar to those I frequently come across in my work. Peyton Manning, Tom Brady and Marvin Harrison are real NFL players, and John Madden and Al Michaels are real sportscasters, but the football game Jack Harris watches is fictional; all other people and companies in this book are fictional, and any resemblance to actual people or companies is coincidental.

I wish you great success as you commit to discovering the dynamic Player-Coach approach to leadership and management. May you discover the joy and power that comes from leveraging the talent around you.

Get the best from your leaders. Give the best of you!

PLAYER-COACH LEADER

LEVERAGE
THE TALENT AROUND YOU

A FUMBLE

Late on a Tuesday afternoon, Jack Harris was at his desk reviewing the status of several large projects when Sara Jacobs came to the door and gave a half-knock. "Jack, do you have a few minutes?" she asked. Deeply engrossed in his paperwork, Jack motioned her in with a grunt.

Sara took a seat and began speaking; every staff member knew you didn't wait to have Jack's full attention to begin a conversation. She jumped right to the point.

"Jack, I wanted to be the first to tell you that I've been asked by Scott Barrymore to lead one of his client project teams," Sara said. "I really respect you and have learned so much about client service working on your team. This is not an easy decision for me, but I would like to take

Scott up on his offer, and I'm asking for your support."

Jack was stunned. This was the third high-talent manager who had left his team to take assignments with Scott Barrymore in less than a year. Why did everyone want to work for Scott? He was a partner with whom Jack got along quite well. But he was no match for Jack Harris when it came to performance and results. What was going on?

For once, Jack Harris was speechless.

RAINMAKER'S BREWING STORM

Recognized as a top producer in the legal and business services firm where he'd been a corporate finance partner for 10 years, nominated to become a Practice Managing Partner—Jack Harris should have felt on top of the world. The Bauer Firm was well respected and had a long history as an innovative and ethical financial services firm. The partners came from both financial and legal backgrounds, which gave the firm a unique position in the market. Much of Jack's success at the start of his career had been due to the credibility and reputation of the firm. It sure didn't hurt to have the Bauer Firm on his business card.

Since joining the firm 10 years ago and making partner soon afterward, Jack had achieved success with his capacity to endure long hours, his intelligence and his creative approach to addressing clients' problems and goals. He had been compensated well and felt great about the level of financial security he had achieved. Jack was a go-getter, and he liked being rewarded for clearly measurable accomplishments. Financial results and a stellar client list were the two things that drove Jack to record-breaking achievement year after year.

Jack had never lost a client in his career; any turnover had been of his choosing, as he continued to attract larger and more sophisticated clients. Clients that did not grow or sustain a strong commitment to excellence were eventually culled and replaced with emerging, responsive and growing companies. Jack's motto was: "You're only as good as the clients you keep."

But lately, he had sensed that something wasn't right. For one thing, the thought of being a Practice Managing Partner of the Bauer Firm was unsettling.

PMPs, as they were called, were a different breed, in Jack's mind. There were eight of them in the firm, managing 270 partners in 30 offices across the country. They were responsible for hiring and developing talent, conducting annual performance reviews of partners, overseeing compensation and succession plans, and executing the firm's strategic plans. They seemed to like wading around in the muck of "people" issues. They were the kind who didn't need specific, measurable rewards for motivation. PMPs wanted power and prestige.

This wasn't for Jack, who thrived on the corporate mergers and acquisitions he helped create. For the past five years, Jack had made his annual sales revenue goal within the first four months of the fiscal year, and he would do the same this year. The only thing he resisted more than managing other people was sitting through mindless, unproductive meetings. Others were better at managing the firm, dealing with the people issues and deliberating over policies and procedures. Jack admired them for it. He would leave the managing to them. That had been his point of view for as long as he could remember, and it had served him pretty well. Jack lived for results, and the firm paid for those results. Life was good.

So if Jack was so sure managing wasn't for him—if the obvious answer was a simple "no, thank you"—why was he struggling so hard with his decision to accept the PMP offer or not? Why did the notion of forever passing up the chance to help lead the firm make him so uneasy? And now there was another reason to feel the ground shake beneath him. Why had three talented managers left his team in less than a year?

The PMP question was a nagging, ongoing concern. But the talent bleeding from his team—that was a crisis.

A STINGING TRUTH

The next day, Jack called a meeting with two key account managers who had been with him for some time. Fred Reynolds, with his background in corporate finance, and Maxine Darley, whose expertise was in business law, both had proven to be very capable account managers for large multinational clients. Jack had depended on them to deliver the services he sold, and he could not imagine what would happen if either of them was planning to make a move. When Fred and Maxine arrived, Jack wasted no time getting right to the purpose for the hastily called meeting.

"Sara informed me yesterday that she will be assuming the lead as project team leader for Scott in three weeks. Obviously, this is going to affect your workload until Sara is replaced. But more important, I need to know if either of you are planning to make a change. I'm beginning to get a little paranoid."

Fred and Maxine looked at each other and back at Jack, but they were not surprised by Sara's decision. In fact, they had known months ago that Sara was looking for a new role in the firm.

The silence was awkward. Maxine spoke first. "I can't say I'm surprised by this news, but it doesn't come at a very good time. My staff is already overextended and I'm not sure how we will absorb the additional work…"

Jack interrupted, "Maxine, what the hell is going on here? Don't punt this. I need answers."

Maxine paused, wondering which of her thoughts she should share. "Jack, let me put your mind at ease. I'm not looking to make any changes. I like the clients I'm serving and you're not that difficult to work with."

Fred interrupted to joke, "I wouldn't go that far, Max." The tension broke as all three laughed. In a more serious tone, Fred continued: "Jack, listen, you are a great example of getting things done and building strong client relationships. That's what everybody admires about you. You interpret 'no' as 'not now.' You are the rainmaker, you work long hours, and no other partner in this firm cares more about meeting the needs of their clients than Jack Harris. But, Jack, because you've always been direct and honest, I think you deserve the same from us. The truth is, people have the perception that your projects and your clients are more important than the firm."

Maxine agreed and added, "Jack, we haven't seen anyone who works for you make partner in nearly three years. People do not feel you are in tune with their needs and aspirations."

Again, Jack sat speechless. He could make no rebuttal.

A TIMELY ENCOUNTER

The Bauer annual partners' meeting was being held at the Hyatt Grand Champions Resort in Indian Wells, California. Jack was looking forward to it: four days of sharing progress reports and strategic planning with colleagues, blended with golf and relaxation, in the foothills of the majestic San Jacinto Mountains. Running late as usual, he raced through O'Hare International Airport to catch his flight to Palm Springs. He was the last passenger on board. Winded, he sank into his business-class aisle seat and got a pleasant surprise: Charles Alexander, senior partner in the Bauer Firm, was sitting next to him.

As the plane reached its cruising altitude and the flight attendants served drinks, Charles and Jack chatted about the record year the firm was having in sales growth.

Charles Alexander had been with Bauer for decades, had served as CEO from 1984 to 1999 and was currently on the board of directors. Jack's fellow partners often mentioned the positive impact Charles had had in their success.

"Tell me, Jack, have you given much thought to the PMP role?" Charles was asking.

Jack knew if he could talk with anyone in the firm candidly, it was Charles Alexander. Charles cared about the future of firm and of the partners as well. No one, to Jack's knowledge, ever questioned Charles credibility in this matter.

"Charles, I'm going to shoot straight with you. I am honored that the firm leadership has confidence I would make a good PMP. But PMPs seem to have skill and patience in dealing with people issues that I do not have. For example, I found out a few days ago that a talented manager in my group accepted a project with Scott Barrymore's team. She was the third manager to leave my group, and I'm not sure why. Maybe you could tell me what Scott has that I don't."

Charles leaned forward in his seat and asked, "Who are you? The Jack I know has never asked such reflective questions. Are you an imposter?"

Jack laughed and admitted that he felt awkward asking for advice. "My concern sounds rather silly, doesn't it?" he asked.

"No, just the opposite, Jack. I'm happy you are willing to ask yourself the tough questions. Your willingness to take ownership of the events says a great deal about you. What happens to us, Jack, is not as important as what happens *after* what has happened."

"Er—what?" said Jack. "Um … it doesn't matter what happens…it matters what…I'm confused."

Charles smiled. "Jack, we can't control what happens to us. It's how we respond and what we do following a defining event in our lives that really matters."

LESSONS FROM A
VETERAN PLAYER

C harles finished his club soda and said, "You know, Jack, we have a couple of hours in the air to kill, and your situation brings up some matters I've spent a lot of time thinking about over the years. Would you mind if I walked through some of the things I've pondered myself, in the context of your question?"

"I would be grateful if you did," Jack answered. *What a lucky draw it was to end up sitting near Charles*, he thought. Perhaps Charles could help Jack understand why people kept leaving his team.

"All right then; just stop me if I run too far afield," Charles said. "I think I've come up with a model of leadership development that ties right in with what you're experiencing. I've noticed that the leaders I respect the most, the ones who are the best of the best, have all gone through four distinct phases in their business lives before they can realize their own full potential as leaders. It could be you're just about ready for a transition into a new phase. But let me start by asking you a question. What type of people do you think make effective leaders?"

"High performers who get things done with excellence and efficiency," Jack said, "decision-makers who are direct and hold people accountable to commitments and deadlines."

Charles let Jack's words hang in the air before saying, "I agree—to a degree. Those are the characteristics of take-charge and results-oriented leaders like yourself. But the problem arises when successful people don't understand that there is more to leadership than expertise and performance—there is also connecting with people in ways that motivate *them* to want to help *you* reach *your* goals. None of us, no matter how good we are, can reach our full potential by ourselves. We need other people to want us to win, and who will help us win. This is just as true at the pinnacle of our careers as it is in the early years."

KEEPING SCORE:
THE EXECUTANT APPROACH

"**W**hen I reflect back on how competitive I was right out of law school, I'm almost embarrassed," Charles said. "Beating the other guy, looking better than others, making sure I produced more work and generated more billable hours than any of my peers—that's what dominated my thoughts every waking hour. And that was a lot of time, because I rarely slept, even on weekends."

"Oh, you too?" said Jack, smiling somewhat ruefully at the memory of the many exhausting all-night work sessions of his younger years.

Charles nodded. " I believed that level of intensity and commitment was required to set myself apart and gain the respect of the partners in the firm," he said. "And I was right. They quickly realized they could depend on me and, consequently, they did not hesitate to push increasing volumes of work my way. The clients loved me because I was the 'no problem' guy who would move heaven and earth to give them what they wanted. And for that commitment I was praised by the head of the firm often and made partner in just under five years."

Charles was too modest to say it, Jack thought, but everyone knew he remained the youngest person in the firm's history to have made partner. Jack had never thought of that record as anything but a solid achievement, something to admire. But here was Charles, sounding as though there was another side to it.

"The truth is, Jack, not much has changed," Charles said. "As a firm, we still recognize and promote the self-initiating, ambitious people who give their all to deliver outstanding results. Those who produce high-quality work in large quantities get the rewards. These people are what I call the executants: high performers, those who get things done, who can execute a plan of action effectively. It is the starting point of leadership, and you have to demonstrate talent at this level if you hope to have the credibility to advance."

"That sounds like me," Jack said, with just a touch of uncertainty in his voice. Was Charles saying it was good to be an executant? Or not? Jack didn't want to pigeonhole himself, but the truth was that Charles had just described him to a T.

"Oh, I'm certain you can relate, Jack. But success at this level can work against the best of us," Charles said. "This is where many high performers get stuck. They think, 'I'll just keep producing for the next 25 years, build a solid book of business, then retire.' But life, as well as the firm, inevitably changes, and the measurements of success get redefined. Those who stay at the executant stage are at high risk of burnout and worse, irrelevance."

Jack was skeptical. "Are you saying that going after new business and playing full out to serve clients leads to failure? It's what I live for."

Charles laughed and continued, "We all start out concentrating on individual achievement; the firm promotes that approach by its compensation structure. But in the bigger picture, a focus on individual achievement should be a kind of rite of passage, not the end of the road. Take a young inventor who becomes obsessed with an idea and labors in his garage for months to turn his idea into a leading-edge product.

He works day and night in obscurity, until one day, he launches the prototype and discovers there is an overwhelming demand for his new gadget. Now it's impossible for him to work alone. He needs the support, talent and resources of many others to realize the true possibilities of his success."

"I see," Jack said, "but there's also the old saying, 'If you want something done right, you have to do it yourself.' If I were that young inventor, I'd have to stay involved. I'd want to choose the factory, approve the materials—I can even see wanting to design the packaging myself."

"I bet you would," Charles said, laughing. "You will always have a personal interest in new business and being involved with clients; that is at the core of our partnership. In our business, partners continue to be players throughout their career. But the position we play and how we execute the play will change as we enlarge our leadership capacity."

EXPANDING THE FIELD: EMINENCE-BUILDING

J ack looked puzzled. "Why change what's working?"

"In the first phase, executants are most concerned with managing their time effectively between new business generation and delivery of services," Charles said. "Then, as you build your client base and begin to leverage the resources of skilled labor, you should begin to think of your contribution to the larger organization. This is the second stage I like to refer to as eminence-building."

"Eminence? What do you mean by that?" Jack asked.

Charles explained eminence-building as a shift in focus, from individual performance to the broader interest of the company. "It's building prominence within the organization by showing you're making decisions based on the good of the firm in its entirety, not just on what's best for you," he said.

Jack thought about what Fred had said to him: *"People have the perception that your projects and your clients are more important than the firm."* He knew it was true. But was it really wrong to feel that way?

He put the question to Charles, who replied, "Some time ago, I met a very successful woman in the medical industry named Lydia. She had invented a remarkable medical device that saved lives. She single-handedly built a business around that device with annual revenues exceeding $40 million. Ten years later, the company hit a plateau it could not overcome and eventually began a decline from which it would never recover. Lydia was removed from leadership by the board of directors whom she had personally selected. Reflecting on her loss, Lydia came to believe she had held on too tightly. No one cared as much for the company, she thought. But then, how *could* anyone care as much for the company when she held every detail of it so tightly in her grip?

"Lydia told me something I've never forgotten: 'I learned the hard way that my reach must exceed my own grasp. And that is only possible when I allow others to contribute their talents to mine, to leverage the talents and skills of those around me, extending the reach of all of us. In my case, my grasp hindered my reach.' Lydia cared for the company, but limited its growth by her need to control and failure to leverage the talents of both her colleagues and management team. Her work in the business distracted her from building eminence and expanding her influence.

Jack remembered reading about the company's difficulties some years before. At the time, he had been mildly shocked; he had considered Lydia, the company's founder, as a sort of role model of the can-do, hands-on style he admired. She had believed totally in the device she had patented; it seemed natural that she had had trouble letting others handle pieces of its development, Jack thought. He said so to Charles.

"To grow as a leader, the executant must exemplify genuine commitment to the health and growth of the organization," Charles said. "As an executant building eminence, you'll be no less motivated by performance, but your idea of 'performance' reaches beyond personal measures into the advantages for the whole organization. At some point in your leadership development, people must come to believe that you care enough about the firm to let go and make room for others. That's when you start to realize, 'I can't go it alone; I need to contribute to my peers and our future as a firm.'"

"I'm still a player, in the game for measurable results, but my responsibility expands and I begin to play for the team win—is that it?" Jack asked.

"Yes. People must want to help you win, but they can't support you in that way until they know you have the partnership or the firm's best interest at heart. They can't trust you to be a good steward of their talent if they can't trust you to do what's right for the firm."

With an uneasy pang, Jack realized that Charles' words echoed what Maxine had said: *"People do not feel you are in tune with their needs and aspirations."*

In a reflective tone, Jack expressed what he understood Charles to be saying: "So you're saying that getting stuck in the executant stage is a serious limitation—even when it looks like success. Eminence is about serving as a model within the firm and letting others know it's safe to help each other win."

Charles said, "Yes—but it's not just within the firm that you should aim for eminence. Visibility as an expert in an industry and in the business community, the level of respect you have among leaders outside the firm: these are also factors in eminence-building. In this leadership stage, you also must contribute thoughtful ideas and insight to the broader community.

"Many leaders of successful companies become isolated," Charles went on. "They let the demands and expectations of their immediate circle box them in. They feel they must remain hands-on. Often this is driven more by ego than true necessity."

Jack sighed. Had he become totally driven by ego, to a point where he couldn't even see it—although, it seemed, his staff could? But then again, were Charles' views simply impractical?

"How do you get everything done if your focus is divided between your own goals and your team's?" Jack asked. "I already put in 80-hour work weeks. If I have to worry about how everyone else is doing, when do I sleep?"

"Leaders who achieve eminence master delegation," Charles said. "They leverage the talents and brainpower of many people. They do this as a matter of course, so it doesn't take much extra time at all. They create environments where their team can function effectively and creatively. Eminent leaders rise above the confines of individual per-formance and begin to define success by the collective success of the people around them."

TAPPING UNREALIZED POTENTIAL: ELEVATING OTHERS

J ack remained somewhat skeptical. It sounded easy, but in his experience, everyone was pretty much out for himself. If he suddenly put others' goals right alongside his own in importance, wouldn't his own goals just get shoved down the priority list? If he was looking out for everyone else, who would look out for him?

He closed his eyes for a moment and pictured the members of his team who had come and gone over the years. Among the images, Sara Jacobs' jumped out. He recalled the way she had impressed everyone during the interview process. She was smart and quick thinking on her feet; from her earliest days at the firm, she had demonstrated great judgment with clients. He remembered Sara's first project. Jack and his team were involved in several high-profile projects in Chicago; they were short-staffed, and the volume of work was mountainous. Between managing the client relationship and working impossible hours himself to structure the deals, the last thing Jack had thought about was Sara, who had just jumped in, taken initiative and sorted things out as she went along.

"Wasn't that delegating? Isn't that what Charles meant?" Jack wondered to himself. But as Jack considered further, he realized that as Sara's workload and client list had increased over time, he had never coached her or invested in her development. Oh, he had performed the perfunctory annual reviews and she had been given generous salary increases. But for the first time, Jack realized that he had not taken a very active interest in delegating assignments to Sara in a way that would have provided for her growth and advancement. The work assignments had simply been dumped on her, and then she was out of sight and mind. It was more like relegating than delegating. Jack had to admit, he only paid close attention to his staff when something went wrong with their assignments.

Jack looked at his watch. Less than an hour left in the flight, and Charles had mentioned four stages of leadership growth. With so much, obviously, to learn, he felt an urgency to make the most of the opportunity to learn from Charles.

"OK, Charles, what's the third level of leadership growth?" he asked. "Once I've stretched to understand how I contribute to the firm and the larger community, what comes next?"

"I think of the next phase, when we elevate those around us, as going from a player mentality to more of a coach mentality: seeing ourselves not only as a player, but as what I call a Player-Coach. Player-Coaches are dedicated to leveraging their experience and talent through other people. Player-Coaches focus on elevating the leaders around them— lifting others up to a higher level of performance than they could achieve on their own. Player-Coaches are surrounded by leaders, not followers."

Jack still wasn't sure he could put this idea into practice. "Charles, this is beginning to sound like management of others and less like making things happen."

"Jack, do you think you will be able to reach your goals by yourself?" Charles asked.

"So far, I've done quite well for myself," Jack shot back.

"But is 'quite well' enough for you?" Charles asked. "Unfettered success happens in direct proportion to your ability to inspire other people, who, in turn, will want you to succeed. When you've created a following of leaders who know you are committed to elevating them, you will have tapped into exponential success. Young potential leaders tend to rise to the expectations of the leaders they respect. Once that respect is gained, they will want you to succeed. Then an amazing thing transpires between you and them: You will discover even more joy in their success than in your own success."

Jack sensed the truth in Charles' words. At the executant level, Scott Barrymore was barely in Jack's league. But in developing talent, Scott was far ahead, and maybe that was one reason managers wanted to work with him. Younger members of the firm clearly knew Scott Barrymore would nurture their careers along with his own; two of them had gone from Scott's team to full partnerships in the past three years. Score: Scott 2, Jack 0.

As the plane began its descent into Palm Springs, Jack pondered what Charles had said and how it related to his internal struggle over whether to accept the PMP offer. He felt he was at a pivotal moment in his career. The decision about the PMP role was bringing him face to face with his core beliefs about leadership. He knew he might never like the administration responsibilities required of a PMP. He had very low tolerance for handholding and preferred working with self-motivated individuals.

But the idea of Player-Coach sounded like an approach Jack could understand, if perhaps not immediately embrace. He knew it was true that his scope of accomplishment would be severely limited if he failed to attract and keep highly talented, motivated professionals on his team. Sara's departure and the candid things Maxine and Fred had said to him made that unavoidably clear.

If he took Charles' comments to heart, Jack would have to make the decision about becoming a PMP in the context of how he contributed to the future of the firm. As a leader in the firm, Jack had always known he had responsibility for developing future leaders; he just hadn't gone about it in any systematic way, nor really considered it integral to achieving his own goals. But if he wanted to be a Player-Coach leader, as Charles had pointed out, he would have to be surrounded by leaders, not followers. And to create those leaders, he would have to put greater emphasis on creating growth experiences for his teammates and to let them learn by doing.

Jack felt he needed to know more. "OK," he said. "We've discussed the executant stage, building eminence and elevating others. What's the fourth phase?"

THE GREATEST LEGACY: BECOMING ESTEEMED

"The fourth stage is more of a lifelong achievement, and it is not something we can attain in and of ourselves," Charles answered. "You might say it is conferred on us by others, and I'm not sure anyone really knows when that magic moment really occurs. It is that period of our lives when we are esteemed by others.

"Esteem is not something you seek to achieve, like status or position," Charles explained. "To be esteemed is a natural outcome of having lived well and contributed to life in meaningful ways. I like to think if we live out the first three stages we've discussed in an exemplary and consistent manner, we will earn a good name and reputation. In my mind, this is the ultimate level of personal satisfaction, a measurement that can only be calculated by the degree to which others desire to imitate our lives."

Charles certainly was esteemed at the Bauer Firm. He always had an open door and took time to explain things to people. Sometimes he just asked the tough questions and sent people away to wrestle with an issue until they had their own solution. Charles had mentored many top executives in companies throughout the country; Jack had met some of them, and they always spoke of Charles with a kind of reverence. Some of them had painful stories to tell of times when Charles had pushed them to their end. But each one spoke of his consistency. They would shake their heads and say, "You will always know where Charles stands on something. You may not like it, but you can count on it."

As the plane arrived at the gate and passengers began gathering their carry-on luggage, Charles invited Jack to join him for the ride to Hyatt Grand Champions Resort.

"When you have passed through these four phases—executant, eminence-building, elevating others and earning esteem—you will be in the best possible position to be a Player-Coach for your teammates," Charles said as the taxi left the airport. "But seeing yourself as a Player-Coach can begin any time in your career. It's up to you."

FROM PLAYER
TO **PLAYER-COACH**

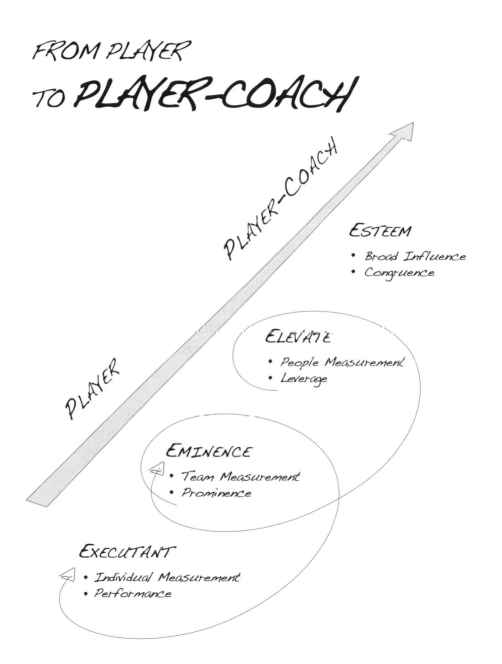

PLAYER-COACH

PLAYER

ESTEEM
- Broad Influence
- Congruence

ELEVATE
- People Measurement
- Leverage

EMINENCE
- Team Measurement
- Prominence

EXECUTANT
- Individual Measurement
- Performance

CHARACTERISTICS OF A COACH

I t was a perfect day in Indian Wells, with an ideal temperature and clear skies. Jack started his day early in the fitness center and was anticipating a great round of golf later in the afternoon. He arrived at the conference center early enough to connect with several old friends before the meeting started—but not too early; waiting around for meetings to start did not suit Jack Harris very well.

Applause greeted the Bauer Firm's CEO, Ken Darden, as he took the stage to deliver the keynote speech. He had led the firm through five difficult years that had seen a major reorganization and a new business model that had involved selling off Private Estate Planning Services, a large retail division that had been a part of the firm since its founding. The transaction meant that many of the partners who had been with the firm for years had suddenly found themselves working for another organization. But it had allowed the firm to focus on its strength of serving corporate clients that were mid-cap and larger in size. The firm had been able to concentrate its resources toward dominance in this market segment, resulting in record-breaking growth and profitability.

"Ladies and gentlemen, the progress we've made this year is because of your great talent, dedication and leadership," Darden began. "This new business model we've embraced as a partnership has required us to inspire greatness among our people and articulate a vision that is worthy of their full commitment and sacrifice. For us to succeed in the future, we all need to think of ourselves as coaches of our top talent in the firm. And for us to be effective coaches, we must prepare ourselves to be coached as well."

This coaching idea was obviously on the minds of the senior partners in the firm, Jack thought.

"There is a leadership crisis in business today," the CEO said, "a leadership crisis that stems from short-sightedness and, consequently, poor coaching of future leaders. Our becoming good coaches will give our firm a distinct competitive advantage and exponential growth, both in the short and long term."

The CEO had everyone's attention as he clicked through a presentation titled "Six Characteristics of Effective Coaches." As the bullet points appeared on the screen behind Darden, Jack found himself recalling moments from his own career that seemed to fit right in with what the CEO was saying:

1. *Great coaches are future-oriented. Performance is important, but what's possible in an athlete tomorrow is more important. Great coaches develop the ability to identify and draw out talent even the athletes may not be aware they possess.*

Jack fondly remembered Howard, his first real boss. Jack could still smell the stale air of that bookkeeping office and feel the oppressive boredom that hung over him. Howard had taught Jack everything he could about how a corporation should document its financial activity. Then one day he walked into Jack's office, sat down on the desk and asked matter-of-factly, "Why are you here?" Jack remembered searching for words and his mind going blank. He didn't know why he was there; it's just where he had ended up after college. Howard had said, "Jack, you've been a real asset here, but this is a way station for you. You need to be out in the world making things happen—creating the transactions, not just documenting them. Learn what you can here, move on—and buy me dinner someday when you're a big shot." They had laughed, but spurred in part by Howard's words, Jack had begun to think seriously about his direction in life. It was the beginning of a trajectory that carried Jack into law school, corporate finance and ultimately to the firm. And, in fact, Jack had bought Howard dinner a few years back at the best restaurant in town. Now he thought, "Howard saw my potential before I even had a clue."

2. *Great coaches are direct and honest. They tell it like they see it. Only then can they help an athlete know what it will take to improve.*

Jack knew exactly what Ken was referring to. It was so easy to take the shortcut when dealing with a staff member who was good, but not great. Such teammates were valuable for getting work done, but often developed bad habits. "So in the short-term interest of client service, we allow them to continue being good at what they do without telling them they could become great," Jack thought. Or, he realized with a jolt, in my case, I tell them nothing at all until they make a mistake—or leave my team.

3. *Great coaches accelerate learning. They remove the clutter and chatter that distract from performance. They direct the athlete to concentrate on a few key strengths and practice those strengths until they can perform them time after time without faltering, even in changing conditions.*

Jack recalled how when Mark Lesage, a rising star in the corporate finance department, had first joined the firm, he was zealous to excel and please. This had led Mark to offer to do anything for his colleagues from researching arcane points of law to fetching coffee. And this, in turn, had caused him, on one important occasion, to miss a key deadline of his own. Mark became so upset about the missed deadline that he became physically ill. Upon his return to work, Jayne Waters, one of the firm's senior partners, had pulled him aside and asked, "What are you trying to prove and to whom are you trying to prove it?" Mark had told Jack at the time it was as though she had pulled back the curtain of his soul and laid bare his fears that he was a fraud, that he would fail in some aspect of his job, that he had to excel at everything and be liked by everyone to be a success. In a series of meetings, Jayne had helped Mark learn to put those fears aside and focus on his areas of strength. One of these was his skill at calming clients who had last-minute nerves before a major deal was to close; his command of details and his personable nature helped clients stay cool so transactions went much more smoothly. Once he began to respect his own gifts and refine them, Mark became one of Bauer's shining young stars.

4. *Great coaches are consistent; this trait, more than any other, builds trust between coach and player. Great coaches can be counted on to be consistent in their values and in keeping their word, and they can be counted on to hold others equally account- able, without exception.*

Jack immediately thought of Charles; surely, he felt, Ken also had thought of Charles when he prepared these remarks on leadership con- sistency.

5. *Great coaches are approachable. Players must always know they can talk to their coach about anything and everything. The coach must be humble enough to be interested in the thoughts and feelings of the player. This is an "other-people-first" philoso- phy of leadership.*

"I'm approachable," Jack thought, relieved to find an area he could feel positive about. "After all, Sara Jacobs didn't hesitate to walk right into my office and announce her decision to leave my team." But then he realized Sara had made that decision right under his nose, without his having seen any sign of it coming at all. Was it possible to be so engrossed in your work that you became unapproachable, even if your door was technically open?

6. *Great coaches explain things, which requires self-confidence and patience. People need to understand why things are expected of them and what the purpose is behind what they're being asked to do.*

Ken had done a masterful job explaining to the partners why it was good for all to sell off the Private Estate Planning group. Anyone else might have caused a mutiny, Jack thought, but Ken had skillfully and patiently taught the partners why it was the right path. By leading his key players to a new way of thinking about the future of the firm, he had led it to a new and promising position in the marketplace.

The CEO wrapped up his speech by calling upon the partners to develop the leaders around them through the power of coaching. "It is the greatest single contribution each partner can make to the future success of the firm," he said. "Life has a way of bringing people into our lives who are supposed to give us something. They are put in our path for growth and learning. I'm certain that if you take a few minutes to think back over your career, you will readily identify mentors and coaches who provoked and inspired you to become a better person. You may even have a couple who were an example of how *not* to do things. Even if you're well established today, you may still have people who coach and mentor you in various areas of your life.

"Do your people see you as a coach? Will they remember you as someone who had a positive and intentional impact on their lives and career? This is important not just for them; this is critical to keep the Bauer Firm healthy and growing into the future. Our future hinges on the investment we partners make into those young men and women who support us."

Jack joined his fellow partners in a standing ovation for Ken Darden. But as he applauded, he wondered whether he would ever be able to put any of the CEO's advice to practical use.

PLAYING DEFENSE

The following day, Jack began to notice a subtle difference from previous years in the business sessions. Leadership and coaching were underlying themes of every session. Words like "collaboration," "collegiality" and the idea of elevating key talent were sprinkled in the presenters' remarks throughout the day.

During the afternoon break, Jack checked his voicemail. The fourth message was from Fred Reynolds. Fred asked Jack to return his call as soon as possible, and his voice had an agitated tone. Jack dialed Fred's cell immediately.

"Fred, this is Jack. What's going on?"

Fred began with a sigh, "I really hate to disturb you during the Partners' Conference, but an issue has come up involving Digital Streaming." Digital Streaming Company was one of Jack's largest clients, representing more than 20 percent of his annual revenue.

"I had a meeting at their office this morning and as I was leaving, I ran into the CFO, David Johnson," Fred went on. "David told me that he and others at Digital were not satisfied with our handling of the Paul Rayburn issue. They continue to question his judgment and want him taken off of their projects immediately."

Paul Rayburn was a young assistant manager who specialized in tax. Paul had demonstrated his ability to juggle multiple tasks and assignments. His greatest fault was wanting to impress partners with his "got it covered" style. He appeared to believe that asking partners for assistance was a sign of weakness. His stock "I've got it" response to questions about the status of jobs left some of his colleagues with a sense of unease, although he was usually on top of his projects—until the Digital incident.

Several months earlier Paul called the Internal Revenue Service on Digital Streaming's quarterly employer tax, explaining that the payment had been made but was incorrectly coded to the prior quarter, and that a written explanation would be forthcoming. David Johnson of Digital had asked Paul on several occasions about the matter; Paul had assured him that it was taken care of. Then Digital Streaming received notification from the IRS of intent to levy for unpaid taxes. Clearly, he had not followed up with the IRS as promised, and he had not kept the client informed. Paul easily resolved the matter without harm to Digital, but his follow through practices were now in question.

Jack felt the Rayburn thing had been blown way out of proportion and he was irked by Johnson's tactics, using Fred to get to him when he could have called directly. "Where did you leave it, Fred? Why does this trifling issue keep coming up? Paul made a mistake, but we caught it in plenty of time."

Fred answered, "I told David you would call him within the next 24 hours. Anything less than a personal response from you would add fuel to his fire."

Jack suppressed his irritation, thanked Fred for alerting him so quickly and promised to call Johnson right away. He scrolled down on his phone to David Johnson's direct number and hit "send."

"David! Jack Harris here. How will I ever repay you for giving me a reason to get out of a mind-numbing meeting?" Jack and David shared a laugh, but both were aware of the underlying tension.

That's what David liked about Jack: He had a way of taking charge and making people laugh. But this time David was determined to not let him off the hook. Many of the senior executives at Digital Streaming had begun to question Jack's level of engagement with their account, and David was beginning to lose credibility with the group for defending Jack Harris. It was time for a talk.

David said, "Listen, Jack, I know you're calling as a result of my little sideline conversation with Fred this morning. Why don't we meet for breakfast next week and discuss this face to face?" They agreed on a day and location.

Jack felt better knowing that he would be able to deal with David's concerns in person after he returned. Client concerns and issues struck Jack at his core. The client always came first, and he prided himself on the loyalty his clients had rewarded him with over the years. To have a key client question his attentiveness was appalling.

The current work at Digital didn't require him to be hands-on; Fred and the other staff members were more than capable of handling things. And he was in tune with the status of the project. But Jack knew the only thing that really mattered was the client's perception.

INSTANT REPLAY

The October sun streamed through the trees into Jack's home study late Sunday afternoon. He had enjoyed being with his family and attending worship that morning. A remark in the minister's sermon, about how every person's work would be tested by fire to prove its quality, had stuck in his mind. He sat alone with his thoughts, pondering the quality of his work and reflecting on Ken Darden's words at the Partners' Conference about being more intentional in the development of leaders.

The restlessness Jack felt about how things were going at work made the minister's words smart even more. He was confident that none of his fellow partners worked more hours than he did, and he was the undisputed leader in billable hours. But he knew that his effectiveness would be severely hampered if he continued to lose staff. The fact that Sara Jacobs, one of the rising stars in the firm, had decided to switch teams had seriously bruised his ego. He entertained the thought that she just couldn't handle the pressure of working on a team as demanding as his, but deep down he knew better. Sara was tireless and the clients loved her. She was one of the brightest, most committed managers he had seen in quite a while.

Jacks thought went to his earlier conversation with Fred and Maxine. He believed they had his best interests at heart, and that's why they had been so candid with their remarks. Jack thought about the perception that his clients were more important to him than the firm. He didn't deny that his commitment to client service was his first priority. If you don't have clients, you have no business. But the health and strength of the firm was essential to providing the client with the best services and resources possible. Jack did appreciate the Bauer Firm and was proud to be a partner. Why wasn't his productivity and reputation for taking care of clients enough?

Again, Maxine's words rang in his mind: "*Jack, we haven't seen anyone who works for you make partner in nearly three years.*"

Jack thought about Charles Alexander's comments on the people side of leadership development, and about the limitations on personal performance when leaders lack the ability to leverage the talents and energy of many other people.

The more Jack thought about his life at work, the more he disliked what he had become. He thought about his strengths and the things he had to do at work that drained his energy and enthusiasm.

Jack reviewed the four stages of leadership Charles had explained to him—executant, eminence building, elevating others, and esteem—and decided he, for the most part, was stuck at the executant level. He was a producer, a strong player, perhaps gaining eminence to a small degree, but he was clearly not elevating the people around him, never mind gaining their genuine esteem.

He decided to take a break from work worries and switched on a football game. The New England Patriots were hosting the Indianapolis Colts. It was a battle between the Patriots' Tom Brady and Peyton Manning of the Colts, two of the best quarterbacks in the National Football League. Sportscasters John Madden and Al Michaels were calling the play-by-play. The game was tied at 10 to 10 in the final seconds of the second quarter and the Colts had the ball on the Patriots' 29-yard line.

Manning, working with no huddle, came up to the line of scrimmage with only 21 seconds on the play clock and surveyed the defense, deciding if the play he'd called would work. Once he saw the defense, he began to bark out a different play, shifted players from one side to the other, changed the protection scheme and then, switching from under center to the shotgun, called the play.

Madden, watching Manning maneuver in those final seconds, said, "Look at this guy—he knows every position on offense better than the players themselves. Even when you talk with the guy, you get the feeling he's half player and half coach."

Michaels called out, "Manning takes the snap, it is up, he airs it out to Marvin Harrison, he's in the end zone, what a catch, he got it…touchdown! Touchdown by Marvin! … and the Colts regain the lead."

Jack sat straight up. "That's it! That's exactly what Charles Alexander meant by Player-Coach. Half player and half coach. I'm the quarterback of my team. I must understand every position my team members are playing so I can coach them for top performance. I can't just do my thing and leave them to play their positions alone. It doesn't work in football, and it doesn't work in business."

He would call Charles right away Monday morning to arrange another meeting. He wanted to pick Charles' brain on the best way to execute as a Player-Coach.

THE GAME CHANGES

It was a few minutes before 10 on Monday morning when Maxine and Fred walked into Jack's office. This would be the first weekly managers' meeting without Sara Jacobs.

Fred and Maxine gave brief updates on the most critical projects they were working on, while Jack listened.

Fred concluded with an overview of the Digital Streaming situation, and Jack asked, "Fred, what are your thoughts on this?"

Fred paused. Then, looking directly at Jack, he said, "I'm just waiting for you to tell me to fire Paul Rayburn."

That was exactly what Jack would usually have demanded. It was his way of sending the client the message that he took such situations very seriously. Even now, he wanted to fire Paul.

But in light of his conversation with Charles and Ken Darden's speech, Jack had decided to try a different approach and see how it felt. He asked Fred, "In your opinion, what is the best way to handle this situation with Paul?"

Fred couldn't believe his ears. If he and Maxine could have read each other's minds, they would have heard the same words: "Be careful, Fred—you're being set up."

Paul was a very talented team member and had demonstrated great potential, both in technical ability and work ethic. He had made a mistake, but clearly not one that should lead to his termination. Fred had resented Jack's demands for firing people in the past, and he felt this was the time to speak up. With the loss already that year of three young managers, the morale of the group would sink to unmanageable lows if Paul were fired. He chose his words carefully.

"Jack, I do not think Paul Rayburn should lose his job over this. Sure, Paul should have followed up his call to the IRS with a written explanation and made sure the deadline was met. But quite honestly, everyone knows that his draft of the letter sat on your desk for some time waiting for your approval. Is it any wonder why Paul forgot to finalize the letter and send it in? He shouldn't bear all the blame."

Fred wasn't sure if Jack was even aware of how often he had let staff members take the fall in order to preserve his reputation with clients. He nervously awaited Jack's response.

Jack turned to Maxine and asked, "Maxine, I would like to hear from you as well."

"Jack, people want to work with you because you know this business and you are a winner," she said. "But the problem is, people are beginning to think that the only person on Jack's team who ever wins is Jack. As I said before, the problem with attracting and keeping people on this team is they learn that advancement is all but impossible. While people admire your work ethic, they have come to believe your only motivation is building your own future and no one else's. A little support from you would not hurt productivity, Jack; in fact, it just might improve our performance."

She, too, waited tensely to see what Jack would say.

Jack's instinct was to defend himself and justify his actions. He didn't believe things were as bad as Max and Fred had described them. But maybe, as with Sara, he had not being paying attention.

Maxine and Fred waited for the outburst of temper they were sure was yet to come.

Finally, Jack spoke. "Thank you for your honesty. So, Fred, you never answered my question. How shall we handle Paul?"

Fred was astonished at Jack's calm, and struggled to find his own. "I suggest we explain the severity of this to Paul and give him a second chance. As for David Johnson wanting him off of their assignments, I recommend that decision be delayed until you can meet with David personally."

Jack asked, "What are you expecting from that meeting?"

Fred figured he had nothing to lose at this point. He responded, "I think you should stand up for Paul and assure David that Paul's work will be closely monitored. Then we make our own decision as to Paul's future on the Digital Streaming team. I would suggest a good starting point would be for you to speak with Paul, Jack, and give him a chance to explain how this happened. He's tormented over what you must think of him."

Jack smiled and said, "You're tough, Fred. But I think your approach is reasonable, and that's what we'll do. Thank you both for being direct and candid with me today. Now, let's get to work."

GAME FACE

J ack arrived early at the club for his breakfast with David Johnson, CFO of Digital Streaming. He was thinking about Fred and
Maxine's words two days earlier. Jack didn't want to admit that
he let staff members take the rap in order to preserve his relationship with clients. Was this really the perception of him among the
team members?

David Johnson arrived, and as they ordered and ate breakfast, they
chatted about Digital Streaming's current projects and potential projects
on the horizon. Jack was the first to bring up the real reason for their
meeting.

"David, your comments to Fred last week were very unsettling. I would
like you to speak openly with me about your concerns."

David did not hesitate. "Jack, Paul Rayburn failed to follow up with
the IRS after having assured me that he had taken care of the matter.
This was one of multiple mistakes Paul has made over the past several
months. We do not want him on our account."

"I understand," Jack said. He was tempted to agree, but Fred's words
were ringing in his mind. "You know that I would never keep an in-
competent staff member on the Digital Streaming team. Our people
are the brightest young professionals in the market, and Paul is no
exception. I had a long talk with Paul. He assumed that the IRS would
suspend all action as a result of his initial telephone call, and that, of
course, isn't what happened. He accepts responsibility and truly regrets
the problems that caused for you and your team.

"I'm as much responsible for this error as Paul. I want to assure you that it will not happen again. I ask that you give Paul, and me, another chance to regain your full trust. Fred will monitor Paul's work much more closely. I would welcome the opportunity to explain this personally to other members of your team, if you feel it would help."

David was amused. He responded, "Who are you? And, what have you done with Jack?" They laughed, then David said, "You must think pretty highly of Paul Rayburn. I've never known you to stick up for a staff member like this before. I will explain this to our team and assure them that you are personally handling the situation. But you and I both know that Paul must be more thorough and accurate going forward. Agree?"

Jack agreed. David moved on to another subject, but Jack was feeling pretty good for taking responsibility and not throwing Paul Rayburn under the bus.

Jack returned to the office looking forward to the meeting he had set up with Charles Alexander that afternoon. He was eager to talk over everything from the Rayburn matter, to the insight he'd had while watching the football game, to the keynote address at the conference.

A CONCEPT CLICKS

nce Jack arrived at Charles' office, he plunged right in. "I found Ken Darden's keynote address theme surprisingly similar to our discussion on the plane. This coaching idea seems to be the management fad of the future for our firm."

"It is the future," Charles said. "We've been talking about it at PMP meetings for some time now. If we do our coaching well, it will be our competitive advantage in the industry. Right now we have a talent shortage, and this will become more critical over the next five years. Our high standards for new hires, coupled with the sheer number of people we will need to handle an increasing volume of business, are on a collision course, especially since fewer college graduates have the specialized degrees we'll be needing."

Jack told Charles about the situation with Digital Streaming and how he was trying to handle it in a new way. "What really still bothers me is why Paul didn't follow through with making the coding correction after telling the client it was taken care of," he admitted. "I can't figure out why such a bright, ambitious guy would make a mistake like that. Why didn't he remind me that he was waiting for approval of his letter?"

"Think back to when you were a young manager," Charles suggested. "Did you ever feel demeaned or demotivated by a partner you were working for?"

Jack felt a rush of unpleasant emotions as he recalled the face of George Turner, a partner with Pratt and Billingsly, P.A., the first firm

Jack worked for just out of law school. To the young, green Jack Harris, everything the senior members of the firm said seemed to carry a hundred times the actual weight of their words, and never more so than in a Monday-morning staff meeting when George decided to make an example of Jack in front of his co-workers. Standing at the head of the long, polished conference table, framed by shelves of leather-bound books, George informed the group that Jack held the record for lowest billable hours for the month. Then, turning to Jack, he asked, "Jack, why don't you tell your colleagues what you're going to do about it?" Jack felt ashamed, angry and helpless all over again, as though it had just happened a moment ago.

Jack told Charles about the incident. "After that, I was no longer motivated to go beyond the expected level of work," Jack said, speaking almost as though to himself. "My attitude changed toward George Turner. I didn't want him benefiting from my hard work. I remember telling myself back then that when I became a partner, I would always empathize with my managers. But I'm guilty of the same behavior. Paul must feel the same way I did back then."

Charles was pleased to see this concept click in Jack's mind. He knew that in coaching, what a person is told is not as effective as what they discover within themselves.

Jack repeated what he had heard John Madden say about Peyton Manning: that he was "half player and half coach."

"Charles, please help me become a good Player-Coach with my team," he said.

"I will do everything I can," Charles said. "As you might have guessed, this coaching concept is a special interest of mine. In fact, I've been asked to conduct a class for the university's MBA program about my research and experience with coaching. So helping you will help me organize my thoughts, too.

"And along the lines of helping each other," he said, "remember this: Peyton Manning may be a superb Player-Coach. But he gets coached himself, too. We'll come back to that, but just keep it in mind that it's a two-way street."

PLAYER-COACH RAPPORT

C harles remembered Jack saying that he did not like managing people and preferred bottom-line types of interaction. But he reminded Jack that for a player to be receptive to coaching, he must respect the coach. Building respect, rapport and credibility is the responsibility of the coach. People can identify leaders who have a genuine interest in them, so the first step toward gaining trust in people is expressing a sincere interest in them.

"I'm not very good at that," Jack said.

Charles responded, "You're probably better at it than you think. You've been quite engaged with me on two occasions now. And with the level of loyalty you receive from your clients, you must have established a significant level of rapport with them."

"Well, that's totally different," Jack said. "My interest in the client is directly proportionate to their potential contribution to my revenue target."

"But when you are in a conversation with the client, do you openly discuss your personal motivation for talking to them?" Charles asked.

"Of course not. That would be insane," Jack replied, smiling at the thought.

"So you have *your own* motive for engaging the client, and that enables you to show genuine interest in *their* business needs," Charles said. "But your motives are never the overt topic of discussion with the client. Likewise, to coach another individual successfully, you must have *your own* motive for coaching them. But rapport can only be achieved if you focus on *their* interest or need. The skills that have made you successful with your clients can have equal impact on your team, if you choose to apply them."

"My commitment to giving the client the best possible service could be the motivation for coaching my team," Jack said reflectively. "If I want my people to give something to the client, I'll have to give it to them first."

"And if they trust you, they will give it," Charles said. "If people know they can depend on you to be consistent in your views and approach to problems, then even if they disagree with you, they will trust you. But beyond trust, sincerity is the foundation of the coaching relationship. Your people must never question your sincerity about investing in them. If you are *only* interested in them for what you can get in the short term, you undermine rapport. Rapport in coaching requires the ability to make your short-term ambition secondary, and bring to the forefront the long-term potential of the person you are coaching."

Jack added, "So it is my role as coach to create an environment that challenges the people whose potential I believe in, and draw out that potential. This sounds much more energizing to me than 'managing people.'"

CONFRONT
EXPOSING HIDDEN TALENT

C harles showed Jack a chart he had taken from his desk, labeled "Player-Coach Game Plan." The word "COACH" was printed in large block letters arranged across the bottom of the page. He circled the word "Confront," which extended from the "C" in "Coach."

"This might be helpful; it's part of my preparation for the MBA class I'll be teaching," he said. "To coach an individual effectively, you need objective first-hand information on that person's capabilities and motivation. As a coach, you want to observe the talent in action and follow up your observations with targeted discussion. I've named that discussion 'confronting' the person."

Jack put his hands up. "One minute, Charles. I'm not interested in doing interventions."

Charles laughed and responded, "Good, because coaching is not therapy, and in my opinion, psychologists do not make good business coaches. There is a significant difference between coaching and counseling.

"What is important here is an appropriate level of awareness of the person's tendencies in specific business situations. As a Player-Coach, you have the advantage of reading the team member's behavior and performance from your first-hand experience with them."

Jack wanted clarification. "Are you saying that as a Player-Coach, I will not necessarily have to do additional management things—just be more attentive to how my team is operating as we serve the client?"

Charles nodded and continued, "You should be able to function in the Player-Coach role quite naturally because of your experience and insight. The difference will be deciding the most effective way to connect with each staff member to accelerate that person's learning."

Jack had flashbacks of moments with staff members when there had been openings for coaching. He had missed them all. How things might have turned out differently if he had taken a few minutes to engage the team member? Sara, for example. Would she still be on his team if he had coached her and shown interest in her professional development? There was no doubt in his mind that things would have turned out differently.

Jack asked, "Confronting starts with me becoming more aware of each individual on my team, being sincerely interested in them and knowing what their talents and tendencies are. Is that it?"

Charles responded, "That's the first critical step. Then, once you've recognized the person's untapped potential, you must let them know you see it, in a direct and authentic way."

Jack smiled, realizing that is what Charles had done with him a few minutes ago. Jack had said he wasn't very good at showing interest in other people, and Charles had suggested, "You're probably better at it than you think." Charles had used a positive suggestion and followed it up by pointing out Jack's success with clients, to deliver the constructive message that under certain conditions, Jack did, in fact, show interest in other people.

"Let me share a story with you—the experience that opened my own eyes to the power of coaching," said Charles. "Several years ago, one of my partners was rather distant with her staff. The door to her office was usually closed. She interacted with her direct reports only on an as-needed basis. During annual reviews, she gave feedback, but it was usually negative. Everyone said the worst career move you could make was working for her.

"Finally, I brought in an outside business coach to help. The coach gathered feedback from everyone around this partner and presented it to her. It was not flattering, to say the least.

"She came to me and told me how embarrassed she was that her partners and direct reports had such a poor perception of her leadership. She shared the report with me and wanted to know if I thought things in her group were as bad as the report suggested.

"I knew in that moment that what she did with that information rested to a large degree in my response. I simply asked, 'Do you believe you can be effective if your colleagues and staff have this perception of you?'

"She left my office deeply troubled, and I could only hope for the best. But a year later, she had managers fighting for the chance to be in her department. So, needless to say, I believe in the power of confronting with a constructive message."

Jack thought he knew which partner Charles was describing: Jayne Waters. She, like Charles, was a leader in the firm, someone others turned to for guidance and ideas. Again Jack thought of the transformation she had patiently helped bring about with Mark Lesage, now an invaluable member of the firm whose affectionate nickname was "the Closer."

Had Jayne really once been headed down a path not that different from Jack's own?

Jack wondered what kind of feedback from his whole team he would get. He knew he could be confrontational. But confronting with the other person's interest in mind, and not just to vent his own frustrations, was a totally different approach.

"What changes did she make to turn things around so dramatically?" Jack asked.

"During the next few months, she continued to work with the coach," Charles said. "She began allowing team members to handle more responsibility on their accounts. Her door stood open. But the most significant was her commitment to bring each manager face to face with talents within themselves, talents of which they were unaware."

"So if confronting is done correctly, it offers a positive launching point into coaching," Jack said.

"Confronting is essential for you to bring a person face to face with limitations or opportunities," Charles said. "If you don't care about the growth and effectiveness of the person, you probably will not confront them. Or you will confront only to correct, and that will come across as overly critical. The key is being sincerely interested in the person so you can deliver a constructive message."

———◆———

ORIENT
INTRODUCING A NEW PERSPECTIVE

 K," Jack said. "Then what?"

Charles gestured toward the second word on his chart: "Orient," which extended from the "O" in "Coach."

"The next critical step in coaching top performers is to *orient* their thinking toward self-discovery," he said. "It is important to restrain yourself from telling people what has become obvious to you. Let them find it out for themselves."

"But I thought you just told me to confront them," Jack said.

"I did," said Charles. "But I meant that you confront them with the behavior or thinking that needs attention, while not offering the solution or fix. For people to willingly commit to any improvement, you need to help them understand *why* they are doing things the way they are."

Hmmm, Jack thought, thinking of the pleasant sunny hours he had spent on the golf course during the retreat in California. *That's like a golfer who must learn a new swing to remain competitive in a sport where the competition is always getting tougher.* He thought about the lesson he had taken with the resort's golf pro. The pro had given Jack a thorough analysis of his swing and showed him how his grip was leaving the face of the club open and causing an ugly slice. The next day, using what he'd learned from the pro, Jack was amazed at how often his ball landed in the fairway with this slight adjustment.

"A coach observes anything that limits the performance of the player—thinking patterns, attitudes, techniques," Jack mused, pondering at the same time whether he might trim a few more strokes off his game if he changed his grip on the putter.

Charles said, "That's right. As you observe your team members, you will become proficient over time at recognizing areas where they are in a rut. You will see things they don't. People get stuck in comfort zones that limit their progress. When you see the limitations, you will have the opportunity to help the player come to the same realization.

"You have told me quite matter-of-factly that people issues are not your forte. Is that correct?"

Jack thought for a moment and agreed, but with a qualification: "I'm okay with self-initiating, productive people. It's the mediocre whiners I have trouble with. When they start whining, it hurts my brain."

Charles asked, "What is it about their whining, as you call it, that irritates you?"

Jack had never analyzed his reaction to people he considered mediocre. What was it about them that frustrated him so?

"I suppose it's their neediness, or maybe their lack of commitment to excellence in their work. At times, I feel like there are some people who just want everything handed to them. I've never had anything handed to me. My success has come from personal initiative and hard work. Why should it be any different for them?

"My success has been the direct result of staying focused and delivering for my clients," he continued. "I know that staff is important, but I never considered it my role to change them in any way."

"But just by sharing the key things you've learned in your own life, you can benefit your team," Charles said. "Let me tell you a story. Several years ago, right after I was elected by the partners to be CEO, I was driving home and feeling the weight of leadership of the firm on my shoulders. A few weeks earlier, my mentor, a man I held in high esteem, had passed away. I was feeling both my deep loss and the loneliness of being the head of the firm. I pulled my car over to the side of the road and sat quietly in the stillness. It was a starry night. I looked up at the constellations, stars of varying magnitudes forming the familiar patterns. I felt myself a powerless speck in a vast universe. The person who had guided me was gone, and now hundreds of others needed my guidance—which I did not feel ready or qualified to give.

"But it occurred to me as I sat there that my feeling of powerlessness was actually a competitive feeling—a comparison with how I saw myself relative to others. I thought I should feel somehow 'better' than them if I were to lead them. Sitting there in my car, it dawned on me: I was just as human as the people I was supposed to lead—but that also meant they were just as human as I was. Rather than having to 'outshine' them, I needed to anchor the pattern we made together—to be the brightest star in the constellation, but not the only one.

"I felt almost as though my mentor had orchestrated that experience for me," Charles concluded with a smile. "It changed my outlook on life. Other people were now looking to me to direct them and to invest in their lives. I had to provide more comprehensive leadership while also helping them shine."

Jack sat silently for a moment. "What you said about feeling competitive hits home," he admitted. "In the past, I've kept people at arm's length by believing that *they* are mediocre, but *I* am not. Are you saying if I had focused more on inspiring them rather than dismissing them as mediocre, I would have had even greater success?"

"Yes. But let's be clear: You are not expected to put something into a person that isn't already there. Look for and surround yourself with people who want to learn and grow, then pour yourself into them. The return on your investment will be astounding and more satisfying than you can even imagine."

Jack was still doubtful. Would he have the time for this?

Charles explained that the most effective approach would be to see it as part of doing business day to day. Coaching high performers is best done in real time, but with patience and a commitment to making sure the player is learning. The real issue, Charles said, was the willingness to change one's approach. For highly competent people like Jack, once the mind was open, the "how" would follow.

ACCEPT
PUT THE BALL IN THEIR COURT

J ack was keenly aware that his attitude toward others was undergoing a shift. He felt somewhat embarrassed that he had been so self-centered and one-dimensional in his approach to business.

To Charles, this stage of the coaching process was the most critical. He knew that no matter how much potential he saw in Jack, the decision to make change and then follow through could only be made by Jack himself. Charles had learned over the years as a Player-Coach himself that getting to this level of leadership—the commitment to elevating others as a success strategy—was an individual choice. Charles thought of several high-potential partners in the past who had chosen not to expand their scope of leadership, and how limited the final years of their career had been. For Jack, he hoped for better. Jack had started strong, but could he make the necessary adjustments to end strong?

Charles directed Jack's attention to the third "Coach" word on his chart, "accept."

"This is the most pivotal point in the coaching experience between player and coach. Once the coach successfully brings the player new information and provides insight for learning, execution comes down to the player. The question is whether the player will accept the demands of learning the new skills or new approach."

"So I, as a coach, have to observe my players' attitudes to determine their potential," Jack said.

"Yes—and accept the limits of that," Charles said. "Acceptance is a two-way street. The player must decide to commit to the adjustments and the coach must accept the player's decision. If the coach ignores the player's own commitment to change, he will find himself very frustrated. There are always the people who are inconsistent and need hand-holding."

"So that's how you keep this from eating all your time," Jack said. "If the coach focuses his energy on the people with a winning attitude, he can avoid getting drained by low performers."

"Would you commit more time to building others if you knew they had the potential to be champions?" asked Charles.

"I would," responded Jack.

"Well, you get to decide that," said Charles. "All it takes is a little observation of your players' openness to new ideas and change. If they do not demonstrate an adaptable attitude, you shouldn't have them on your team."

Charles knew the question remained: Would Jack be flexible enough himself to consider changing the way he ran his business?

Charles paused and then asked, "Jack, how would you describe the probability of successfully changing your approach?"

Jack was caught off guard and searched for the appropriate response. He had been open with Charles in the past, so he decided to share his recent conversations with Max and Fred. "Well, to be honest, I've recently had some unflattering feedback from two of my key managers. As I've mentioned before, we've lost a number of very talented people this year. It has been brought to my attention that working for me is seen by some people as career suicide. Unfortunately, Charles, history proves they're right."

Just sharing that makes me feel better, Jack thought. *I hope Charles doesn't lose respect for me. But, either way, I must accept his message and take responsibility for changing in the future.*

CONNECT
CREATING NEW PLAYS

C harles smiled and said, "Jack, your willingness to talk about this and not be defensive speaks volumes about the kind of person you are. You just passed the acceptance phase with flying colors. Now, you have the opportunity to create a new reality.

"That brings us to the fourth step in our Player-Coach model," he said, pointing to the word extending from the second "C" in "Coach": "Connect."

"Changing our approach in business, management, leadership or relationships is most effective when we connect with others so we can focus our work on a shared outcome," Charles said. "'Collaborate' and 'concentrate' would fit here too, but 'connect,' to me, speaks better of leadership. It's active and implies linking things together that may or may not be similar, such as the talents various people can bring to a project."

"Are you suggesting I need others to help me change?" Jack said.

You really are an individualist, aren't you? thought Charles. He knew Jack's independence had enabled him to succeed, but he also knew it now threatened Jack's future and those of the people around him.

"The issue is not whether you need help making changes in your approach," he said. "It's the quality and sustainability of the changes you decide to make. And if a person has the benefit of the talent of several people they respect, the likelihood is much greater of a change standing the test of time. It is the principle of that Hebrew proverb, 'Plans fail for lack of counsel, but with many advisers they succeed.' "

The word "connect" bothered Jack. Could he make this adjustment, harnessing his goals to others', and what kind of impact would it have on his business? One thing was for certain: He may be lacking in the development of his staff, but he was the top producer in the firm. Would it really be possible to achieve a significantly higher level of success if he became more proficient at developing and coaching people?

Looking skeptical, Jack responded, "Charles, I've always been a pretty independent cuss. I've had to be. But I want to get to the next level of success and, believe it or not, I do want my people to succeed as well. So my opportunity is to move from an individual performer mentality to building and leveraging the talents of those around me. Is that correct?"

"Jack, in this matter of connecting, what I'm referring to is your ability to engage other people for your benefit. Remember the night I told you about, just after my mentor died, when I sat and looked at the stars? They were just billions of glimmering specks until someone long ago saw connections; then some stars became part of constellations that travelers could navigate by.

"You have an all-star team of your own; you need to see where each member shines best so you know how to use them in the pattern, the team, you're creating together. But first, you have to acknowledge that they *do* shine—that they have talents and wisdom you may lack. Demonstrating this level of openness personally is essential for you to create it on your team."

"Makes sense—I can't give others something I haven't mastered myself," Jack said.

"Exactly," Charles said. "Connecting is tapping into the brain trust of others' experience and wisdom. It means going beyond your personal agenda and benefiting from considering the objectives and resources of others."

"How is this done on a practical level?" asked Jack. "I mean, the demands of serving our clients don't afford me the luxury of extended periods of time for being reflective and philosophical. Help me out here."

"It just means asking who can provide you with resources to achieve your goals," Charles said. "It means understanding the obstacles you'll encounter and identifying people who can help you overcome them. For example, you might ask those managers who gave you the feedback about how you could be more effective as their leader. Or, you might consider me as a resource for conversations like we're having today.

"In the meantime, think about being receptive to new ways of doing things—ideas that come from others. Try to see yourself from the outside as much as possible; it will help put your own wishes into a context that includes others."

Jack thought about his relationship with Fred and the situation with Paul Rayburn and Digital Streaming. *I was really out of touch with what Fred was dealing with and his true feelings about me. What if I had been more connected? Things would have been handled appropriately and the client would not have had to send me a message through Fred.* Although he had always been aware of how others affected him, Jack never really considered how he personally affected others. It was something to ponder.

Charles was aware that Jack was deep in thought and it was the perfect time for Jack to commit to changing his leadership approach. So Charles asked, "Jack, from our discussion, what do you feel are the key ways you could improve your effectiveness as a partner?"

Jack responded without hesitation. "First, be more aware of my direct reports. Show interest in their professional growth by using key situations as learning opportunities for coaching them. Second, be more open to others' objectives and demonstrate a more collaborative approach with people. The size of my book of business does not allow me to be the only player; if I'm a Player-Coach, I can elevate other players and draw on their talents."

Charles noted that Jack's countenance was brighter and his focus was clear. He said, "Jack, these are your areas where you can become more connected to the people around you. If you put these ideas in the form of action plans and focus on them daily, your leadership effectiveness will be greatly enhanced."

HOPE
POTENTIAL FOR FUTURE WIN

harles glanced at his watch and was surprised that his conversation with Jack had lasted nearly two hours. He walked over to the refrigerator to get a bottle of water, offering Jack one as well.

"I have a four-thirty meeting, but I really want you to share with me the last step," Jack said.

Charles pointed to the last word on the "Coach" chart: "Hope."

"Every human being searches for hope," said Charles, "hope for success and a future that is fulfilling."

Jack was amused. *I never knew we had a philosopher among us*, he thought. "Hope? That sounds abstract. What does hope have to do with real business? 'Sure hope things turn out.' Seriously?"

Charles laughed. "Hope is not just wishing. Hope is expecting a return on your investment and effort. You show up at the office every day and call on your clients to achieve what outcome?"

"Results," Jack said.

"Exactly. You put forth an effort and employ your talent for financial results. So do the people who work for you. They work to fulfill their personal financial goals and security for their families. What else?"

Jack thought for a minute and responded, "Bonuses?"

Charles smiled. "You could say that. People want to be rewarded or acknowledged for their commitment and productivity. But there are deeper and more important motives. People need to know they have a position to play on the team, a reason to play the game.

"If you decide to change your approach—the way you interact with your team—you will do so only if you determine there is something in it for you."

Jack smiled. "Okay. You've got my number. But what's wrong with a little enlightened self-interest?"

"Nothing," Charles said. "All of us are motivated to make changes by either a personal goal, something we want, or a fear, something we must avoid. I see my role as advising and inspiring people to learn. The more people I inspire to increase their knowledge put that new knowledge to work, the more successful I feel."

Jack listened carefully, while part of his mind went back again to Sara Jacobs' decision to work for Scott Barrymore.

Charles continued, "The power of creating hope in your top performers will be realized in two significant ways. First, you will increase the possibility of tapping into the latent talent of your people. Everyone, no matter how ambitious, has undiscovered talent and ability. Successful Player-Coaches have the ability to expose this talent and create an environment where it can flourish. The second benefit has to do with discretionary talent. This is talent and creativity that every team member possesses, but that can never be coerced or bought. It is the energy and effort given willingly and without reservation because they believe in the mission or the person they are supporting."

"So, the aim of coaching my team is to inspire hope for what is possible for them and our group," Jack said. "Charles, my team and I are about to raise the bar on revenue growth, aren't we?"

"That's it, Jack," Charles said. "And, as we discussed earlier, you will reap stage three rewards of being a leader who elevates others.

"By the way, I think you're ready to consider using an executive coach," Charles said.

"Why should I use an executive coach?" Jack asked. "Aren't they for underperformers, just to show them how to get in the game?"

Charles laughed and said, "Well, I've had a coach for years and I don't consider myself an underperformer."

"Really? *You* are coached?"

"Yes, I am," said Charles. "In fact, I make few key decisions without engaging my coach. A third-party coach is not as emotionally connected to the firm and that enables them to bring objectivity to sensitive situations and decisions. It's kind of like when we were talking about Peyton Manning, remember? Coaching, to be truly effective, has to be a two-way street. The coaching I get helps me be a better Player-Coach for others."

Charles explained the difference between players in business and players in professional sports. "In business, we rarely think about coaching our top performers. If we do engage a professional coach, it's usually, as you mentioned, to address poor performance or solve conflicts. Our mindset is more counselor than coach. But in professional sports, top performers would not think about competing at the levels expected of them without a coach. They seek out skilled coaches who can observe their game and help them continue to hone strengths for increasing advantage over their opponents. The difference is that athletes are use to being coached. They are receptive to new information and open to changing or making adjustments to their approach. Business leaders who are serious about keeping that competitive edge should take note. If athletes know the benefits of coaches, so should top business leaders."

Jack thanked Charles for his time as he made his way to the door and his next meeting. Jack knew he had to commit to becoming a stage three leader, one who elevated the people around him. His future depended on it. He couldn't help but blame himself a bit for just now coming to an understanding of the importance of investing in others. Thank goodness, Charles had gained that understanding long ago, and now was able to help coach Jack as he expanded his view of his role as a manager.

That MBA class Charles is planning is going to be amazing, Jack thought. *I feel like I've been thinking so much lately, it's almost like I've earned another graduate degree myself.*

PLAYER-COACH LEADER MODEL

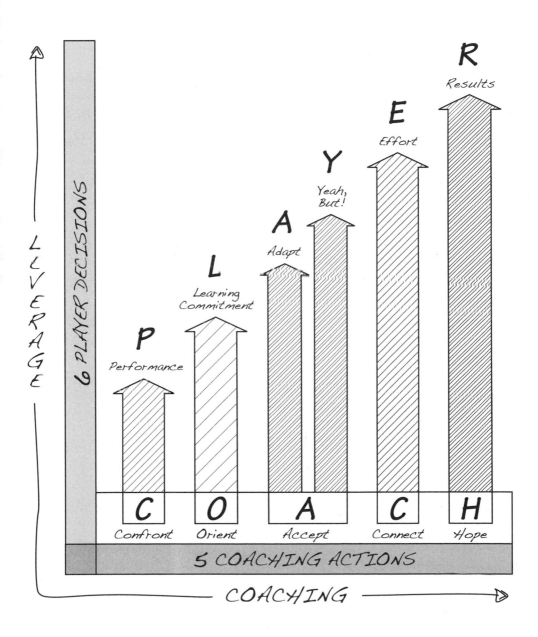

THE 'NEW JACK'?

Max stepped into the Starbucks in the lobby of the Bauer Firm office building for her daily fix of triple non-fat grande latte. As she placed her order, Fred walked up in line behind her. The barista called out, "Hi, Fred, are you having the usual grande caramel macchiato?"

"Of course," Fred replied.

Max turned to him and said, "Predictable, aren't we?"

Fred laughed. "Yes. But when it comes to my coffee, I prefer to call it consistency."

Max asked Fred if he had a few minutes to talk before heading up to the office. She spotted a quiet table tucked away in the corner and waited for Fred to join her.

Fred asked, "So, what's on your mind this morning, Max?"

"Jack Harris is on my mind," she said. "Have you noticed a difference in him the past three weeks, or is it just me?"

"Difference? Like what?" Fred asked.

"I have never known him to show so much interest in what I think about solutions for client matters," Max said. "He seems to be less prone to declaring ultimatums. He seems to show a genuine interest in my thoughts and ideas. It just isn't like Jack."

Fred thought about his recent interaction with Jack. "You know, come to think of it, he did follow my suggested action on the Paul Rayburn issue. In fact, he did better than that. He took responsibility for the mistake with the client, David Johnson, and for the first time that I can remember in a long time, he didn't let a staff member take the hit to protect his image."

Max responded, "Really? This Sara Jacobs situation must have really gotten to him."

Fred laughed. "I think your comment about people feeling that 'the only one on Jack's team who ever wins is Jack' had more to do with it. I couldn't believe you were actually saying that to his face."

Max said, "Well, he asked. And you know me; I tell it like it is. I'm glad that you are noticing similar changes in Jack. Let's hope this is the new Jack. Anyway, we had better get upstairs. Don't want to be late for the staff meeting."

"Not today," Fred responded. "Jack will be introducing Sara's replacement, Richard Wainwright, to the staff. I think he's going to be a good addition to our team."

Max agreed, but added, "I hope he lasts."

PUTTING COACH INTO PRACTICE

S everal days later, Fred sat at his desk preparing for his meeting with Jack Harris. He was deep in thought about how out of character it was for Jack to request a meeting to discuss the progress of a specific staff member. Jack had asked him for an update on Paul Rayburn's performance over the past several weeks with Digital Streaming. Fred was impressed that Jack was showing an interest in the staff, but he wasn't sure what it meant. What was he up to?

When Fred walked through the door into Jack's office, Jack looked up from his work right away, acknowledging him with a warm greeting. He came from behind his desk and offered Fred a chair at the table in the corner of his office.

"Fred, I asked you to stop by today for a couple of reasons," he said. "First, I want to express my appreciation for the quality and consistency of your work. You are very thorough and I am always assured our clients are getting exceptional service when you are the lead. Thank you."

Fred was in shock. *What have they done with Jack? Wow! Did he just pay me a compliment? How should I respond? Is Jack about to fire me?*

"Thank you," he said. "I'm not sure what to say, but I appreciate your comments. Your view of my work means a great deal to me."

Jack continued, "The second thing I'd like to talk about is how you feel Paul is doing at Digital since our encounter with David Johnson."

"Paul was very troubled by the whole situation and took personal responsibility for the filing error," Fred said. "He never tried to pass the buck or make excuses."

Jack was pleased to hear that and asked, "Did you do what we discussed?"

"Yes, I listed the things he should pay more attention to going forward," Fred responded.

Jack was about to move on. But then he thought, *Wait a minute—that was a pretty general answer to my question. Has Fred been totally honest with Paul and put the measures in place we had agreed on?*

"Fred, did you put Paul on 90-day probation with the measurable performance improvements, as you explained them to me?"

Fred met Jack's eyes and said, "OK, I did talk to him about the probation and explained that one more mistake and he would be pulled off of that project. He knows that it may even jeopardize his job at Bauer. But, Jack, when he accepted responsibility and seemed so sincere in his promise to be more careful, I just didn't think it was necessary to impose the performance improvements. He felt really bad about the whole thing."

Jack wanted to start pounding on the table. His could feel the anger coming to the surface. *How could Fred be so casual about this? After I had given my word to David Johnson that we were taking specific internal measures to prevent this from happening again?*

But then Jack reminded himself of the COACH model Charles and he had discussed. *Here is a coaching opportunity, a chance to invest in someone that is important to the team and our clients. I must confront*

Fred constructively at this moment.

Jack paused, then asked, "Fred, do you feel you have been fair to Paul and to the rest of our team by not holding him accountable to clear performance improvements?"

Fred thought for a moment and said, "I suppose not."

Jack asked, "And have you considered the potential negative impact on our client relationship for failing to follow through on what we promised? I assured David Johnson he wouldn't have any more problems from Paul Rayburn. How can we make that assurance if we fail to put this accountability in place and measure Paul's progress?"

Fred responded, "I understand, Jack, but Paul felt really bad and assured me he would do better. I think he was really sincere. But you are right about the client's trust. I'll admit to thinking more about Paul's feelings than the client's expectation. Thanks for pointing that out."

Jack saw the opportunity to re-orient Fred's view of how to effectively manage people and decided to pursue it, saying, "Fred, as Paul's manager, and as the supportive person you are, is it possible that you are being *too* supportive and missing an opportunity for his development? Will Paul be a better professional because of your understanding — or have you sent him the message that there are no consequences for poor performance?"

Fred said, "That's an interesting perspective, Jack. I've never thought it was possible to be too supportive of someone, but I suppose you have a point. Not raising my expectations of Paul and holding him accountable to a higher performance standard could be viewed as taking the path of least conflict. And, in this case, Paul misses the learning opportunity that the performance accountabilities would provide."

Jack was thinking, *Fred's view of avoiding confrontation has now been oriented toward Paul's development and away from how Fred feels about Paul. Now, let's see if he will accept this new viewpoint.*

"Well said, Fred. This is less about how you feel toward Paul and your desire to be supportive. It is really about your commitment to invest in Paul's growth, even though it makes you feel uncomfortable and may even require a little more of your time and energy. So, will you embrace this idea and do what's right for Paul?"

Fred thought, *How long has Jack been aware of my tendency to put my comfort ahead of doing what's right for the people I manage? This is a new approach for Jack as well. I can't believe he's taking the time to make me think about this.*

"Of course, Jack, I accept responsibility for doing the right thing for Paul and will follow through with him this week. I do want to help Paul grow and live up to his potential. I guess I just never thought about the importance of expectations and accountability as a growth opportunity. That really puts a productive emphasis on something that can be viewed as punitive."

"Excellent, Fred," said Jack. "Caring sometimes means caring enough to deliver the difficult message. Now, I want to ask you how I can help. I should not have left this in your court alone in the first place. What do you need from me to be successful with Paul? How can we work together to get the best from him?"

Fred almost fell to the floor in shock. Jack Harris was offering his support and assistance. Trying not to look completely stunned, Fred replied, "No, I mean thanks, Jack, but I will take care of this. And if I need your input I will be sure to ask."

Now connect, Jack thought. *Make sure Fred sees I am part of his actions just as he is part of mine.* We're a team. "OK, but you are not alone, and I want you to let me know if there are any issues I can help with," he said. "I want to see Paul grow from this experience. Let's agree that you will give me an update every 30 days on Paul's progress until we both are confident that he is performing at his best."

Fred agreed. With a smile on his face he stood to leave, saying, "Jack, this has been a great meeting today. To be honest, I was not looking forward to coming here, but this has been terrific. Thank you for the time and input."

Jack leaned back in his chair and reflected on how productive the conversation had been and how pleased he felt. He glanced at his watch and was surprised to see that the entire chat with Fred had taken only a few minutes. To arrive at a productive and positive outcome, to help two employees move toward greater success *and* to feel he had grown from the interaction himself: all that had taken less time than Jack, in the past, would have spent blowing up, pounding on his desk and chewing someone out. And instead of winding up with a big headache — and possibly a fired employee to replace — he had hope for both Fred and Paul, as well as for his own leadership effectiveness. This was the fifth step in the COACH model: hope. Jack's mind and heart were flooded with assurance that his team was about to achieve more success than they ever had before.

Perhaps Jack would always care most passionately about cultivating his book of business. But it dawned on Jack that resolving this "people issue" had actually been satisfying—even fun, in a way. Surely he had grown past the limitations of being completely stuck in the executant phase. He had elevated Paul, Fred and even himself by approaching the Digital problem as a Player-Coach. Was it possible he would someday be as esteemed as Charles Alexander?

Jack's telephone rang and he picked it up.

"This is Ken Darden. How goes the battle?"

Instantly, Jack knew what the call was about. Ken wanted his answer on the PMP role.

Jack retorted, "Battle? Didn't you hear? I won it single-handed." They both laughed.

Jack continued, "Ken, I never thanked you for the excellent keynote speech you gave at the Annual Partners Conference. I took the challenge very seriously, although I must say the idea of coaching for competitive advantage has taken me some time to absorb. A few personal experiences I've had recently have opened my mind to the possibility."

Ken responded, "Thank you for the kind words. I got a mixed response to my challenge, but I do believe our firm must be the undisputed leader in the area of developing new talent and creating opportunities for them. That's how we'll stay out front.

"The reason for my call, Jack, is to get your thoughts on serving as one of our firm's Practice Managing Partners. Where do you stand?"

Jack had known this moment would come, but he had a much better attitude toward the possibility than he had had when it was first presented to him.

"Ken, initially I wasn't sure about whether or not the PMP role was a fit for me. In retrospect, I can see I needed to think about the whole idea of leadership, of what kind of leader I could be—or if I could be one at all. If you would be willing to have dinner with me one evening, I'd like to share with you what I've been thinking recently. Would you accept my invitation?"

"I would love to, Jack," Ken replied. "Let's get a date on our calendars."

PLAYER-COACH LEADER
GAME PLAN

COACHING TO WIN

I n our story, Charles Alexander used a growth scale to help Jack Harris understand that every phase of life and career will lead to a future state. The question is, will that future state be fulfilling and esteem-building, or not?

Charles knew that if Jack did not grasp his overall placement on the progressive scale, he would never be able to appreciate the impact of his interaction with other staff members. We progress up the scale toward a place of esteem through personal assessment of our approach to life and business.

There are four stages of development through which we must navigate to become a successful Player-Coach. These are dynamic and are shaped by life experiences. At each stage, life will present us with the choice to advance or digress. Progress will be determined by our response to the people and situations that challenge us and offer us opportunities to grow.

Executant. The executant is the individual performer who seeks to achieve personal goals without constraints from others. The measurement of success is the attainment of individual goals and personal productivity. At the beginning of a career, opportunity to advance is determined by the individual's ability to produce results. It sets the tone of a person's business life. It is the most basic level of leadership; once success at this level has been demonstrated, the expectations will begin to shift. You are a big producer, but are you aware of those around you?

Eminence. The ability to expand your reach and influence is about building eminence within the organization you serve and the market in which you operate. Eminent leaders are skilled at achieving objectives in ways that please others and increase their own credibility. They demonstrate genuine commitment to the organization, and their decisions advance the firm. To build eminence requires the skill of leveraging the talents and brainpower of many people. The result is big-picture thinking, and success will be measured by the productivity of the team, not just individual performance.

Elevate. Leaders who lift the people around them are positioned for the highest satisfaction and work productivity. They seek to achieve their goals through effective organization and mobilization of many people. The measurement of success is a people measurement determined by the reward of helping others reach their full potential. Those who elevate others will attract high performers, and the word will spread that this is a leader whose people enjoy personal advancement and growth.

Esteemed. Congruence is when "what I do" and "who I am" are in alignment. This level of leadership is the outcome of having lived the other three levels well. A productive life founded on building eminence and elevating others will result in people holding you in high regard. This level is conferred by others and cannot be forced or demanded. Esteemed leaders consistently demonstrate all-win benefits for everyone within their sphere of influence. That influence becomes far-reaching for those who have been true to themselves and lived a principle-centered life.

Every decision you make, how you see things, the way you interact with people—all these determine whether you achieve your highest destiny.

Going through life as an individual player or skillfully leveraging the talent around you will produce significantly different outcomes. Which approach is best for you? Will you become what you might have been?

Two barriers to be managed:

Two barriers must be managed that may not appear to be barriers at all at first glance. They are your own competence and success.

Competence. Sometimes it's the greatest threat to reaping the benefits of change and growth. It is possible to become so competent at what you do that you begin to believe you're the only person who can do it well. Or you might think that because you are capable of doing something, you are obliged to do it. When this happens, you have become a victim of your own competence.

Success. Success is often a barrier to change and growth. Success can breed possessiveness and feed control needs, causing you to shut others out. It usually manifests itself in a lack of patience for mentoring others and fear of losing what you've acquired or accomplished.

You may ask, "Why should I take the time and energy to coach young talent?" After all, your firm pays you on sales and growing your book of business, not holding the hands of junior staff. And your success has been achieved largely by your own sheer will and personal competence. There are two good reasons for committing to the development of your people. One, the rewards will produce success that is orders of magnitude greater than any success you might achieve as an individualist. Two, the personal consequences of not raising up the next generation of talent will rob you of the satisfaction and legacy you deserve.

Consider these five rewards for coaching young talent:

1. You extend your reach by leveraging the talent of other smart people.

2. People will help you win and will want to see you win.

3. You'll benefit from the contribution of discretionary talent — you'll get more from others than you can pay them for.

4. You'll be better able to provide exceptional client service and to maximize use of resources.

5. Being surrounded by a depth of talent and expertise in which you are confident gives you a competitive advantage.

Consider these three consequences of *not* coaching young talent:

1. *Maxed out! You may fall short of your potential because you do not have the right people necessary to support you.*

2. *Burned out! Workload and an impossible schedule leave you stressed and ineffective.*

3. *Tuned out! Peers and partners view you as not contributing to the future of the organization and as driven only by your self-interest.*

You are a player who loves being in the game and delivering the big win. That's great, but how you do that must change over time. You can still be in the game, but you may find you have greater success if you develop the ability to coach while playing the game. You do not have to get bogged down in hand-holding to be a Player-Coach. You do not have to devote hours and hours of extra time. The Player-Coach Leader model presented here will offer you a way to think about how you can continue to do what you love while raising up great leaders around you.

PLAYER-COACH PHILOSOPHY

Player-Coach is about taking a coaching approach to management and to serving your clients. Sometimes it's helpful to describe what something is *not* to understand it better, so let me give it a shot.

Player-Coach is not…

…Becoming less productive

…Command and control

…Telling others what to do

…Listening to brain-numbing complaints

…Soft stuff

…Administration

…Hand-holding

…Doing others' work for them

…Fixing problems or broken people

…Training

…Skill development

…Therapy

…Counseling

…Tolerating mediocrity

The Player-Coach Leader philosophy is about ***getting the best from your leaders by giving the best of you***! The principles of the philosophy are as follows:

1. **Engage for advancement.** Development of other people re-quires the willingness to engage and provide direct feedback when things are going well and when they are not going so well. The fear of losing talent can cause the best of leaders to procrastinate dealing with low performance issues. The irony is that the unwillingness to confront a person who isn't performing at his or her best will often actually result in loss anyway. Having a clear objective for a confrontation will con-trol risk and increase the probability of success. Player-Coach leaders are willing to be direct because they care and they see opportunity for growth.

2. **Have a sincere motive.** Every decision on the Player-Coach's team will be made out of genuine concern for that person and/or for the advancement of the team. Player-Coach leaders suspend their per-sonal agendas when coaching their talent and become totally dedicated to fact-based performance decisions.

3. **See potential in talent.** The Player-Coach believes there is untapped ability in the players around them. (If they don't have that belief, they get different people.) They are dedicated to mining that potential daily. Effective Player-Coaches expect performance that challenges young talent to stretch and accomplish tasks they don't even realize they are capable of.

4. **Listen with empathy.** The discipline of empathizing with your team members is critical for building credibility. Player-Coach leaders consider the implications of others' emotions when it comes to motivating and understanding their people. They are able to leverage those emotions for progress.

5. **Promote solution discovery, not quick fixes.** Making a decision for another person exempts that person from responsibility for the decision and impedes growth. Player-Coach leaders will engage a player in exploring the best possible solutions and will offer options, but only on rare occasions will decide a course of action for someone.

6. **Expose mental limitations.** Personal development is only possible when you come face to face with false personal beliefs. Player-Coaches listen and watch for areas where their players hold back and settle for security or hide in comfort zones. Once they observe mental limitations in their players, Player-Coaches find creative ways to grab the attention of those players and jolt them into new patterns of behavior.

FIVE STEPS TO COACH FOR SUCCESS

Confront: Deciding to engage individual team members to get the best out of them and hold them accountable is the most critical step in becoming an effective Player-Coach. There are plenty of reasons *not* to do this. I have observed some of the most talented and capable leaders avoiding this level of interaction with their people; this is usually for one of three reasons. There are highly introverted, analytical leaders who suffer from low interpersonal skills and possess a high preference for tasks. They can become so technically driven and inwardly focused that they find people issues ambiguous and stressful. Highly driven and dominant leaders just move too fast and furious, and are not always paying attention to the kind of people they are surrounding themselves with. They end up hiring warm bodies to fill slots in a staffing chart out of low patience for due process and fact-finding. Finally, those who are highly supportive and amiable by nature are at risk of being overly patient and too willing to accept excuses.

Whatever the reason and regardless of personal tendencies, it is important for every leader and manager to adapt to confronting people to increase their effectiveness. That must be followed up with progress reviews and ongoing adjustments.

The goal of effective confronting is to raise the player's awareness of his or her performance—to heighten attention to areas of strength and opportunity. Confronting does not have to be negative. Confronting is simply demonstrating awareness of those around you and your commitment to engage them directly for their growth and productivity. It is impossible to manage or lead someone if you are not willing to be direct.

Confronting involves three basic actions:

1. Active observation (willingness to be engaged).

2. Direct explanation (state desired outcomes plainly).

3. Constructive messaging (how the person might be more effective).

Orient: The people who work for you fall into set patterns of thinking and acting that sometimes need to be addressed so they can improve their effectiveness. These set patterns are commonly referred to as "comfort zones." These habits are natural tendencies that determine how people approach their work. Research has shown that people default to their comfort zones when they encounter new or challenging situations. This can work for them or against them. Actively observing how people respond to these challenges provides the framework for coaching them to become better performers, and improves your likelihood of building an effective team.

Sometimes these comfort zones restrict progress and limit a person's ability to see opportunities. It has been said that the thinking and behavior that makes you successful in one stage of life can actually hinder your future success. Thinking you can keep doing the same things and achieve higher levels of success can backfire on you. Sustaining success and reaching higher goal levels requires new approaches that fit the desired objective. It is the role of the Player-Coach to identify comfort zones in people and take action to reorient their outlook.

The Player-Coach, having observed habits that are limiting a team member's progress and confronted that person with the limitations of continuing that behavior, is now able to reorient that person by presenting different ways of approaching problems and opportunities. For example, if you have a manager who is task-oriented and seems to ignore the interests or needs of other people, you can challenge that manager to think more broadly about the situation. You might ask that manager to consider the potential for increased success if other key people supported his or her view. In doing this, you make the manager think about other factors than just completion of the task at hand.

Sam was a very talented chief financial officer who had alienated himself from other members of the management team. This was unfortunate because Sam's view—that this team needed to do a better job increasing sales and managing costs—was on target. However, Sam engaged the other vice presidents with anger and hostility. When he would address his peers in staff meetings, he would become very emotional and attack others. They, as you might expect, returned the favor.

After spending several weeks with the team and coaching them individually, I learned that the team respected Sam's financial expertise, but just couldn't deal with his verbal attacks. He had discredited himself with his approach to the point that the team could no longer listen to anything he said. Even if it made absolute perfect sense, if Sam proposed the idea, it was DOA.

I explained this to Sam, hoping to help him understand what his behavior had cost him, and asked, "How come you feel the need to address everyone with such anger?"

He grinned and said, "Because if I'm nice to these guys, they will think

I'm OK with them taking advantage of this company, and I'm not."
To Sam, being nice to his peers made him an accomplice in their poor performance.

I countered, "But, Sam, you have alienated yourself and you have no influence. Your behavior is not producing change, and you are paying a severe personal price. If you care about the company, shouldn't you do what it takes to be heard so you can influence the others toward change?"

It took a few conversations, but Sam began to understand that his approach was only making matters worse. When he began to make changes, the team responded positively, allowing Sam to become a part of the solution and not the problem. Sam's orientation, his core belief about how to get different results from his peers, had to change, and it did. He made fewer declarations in meetings and genuinely listened to others. He asked sincere and probing questions without taking verbal jabs when people answered. Within six months the entire team had recognized that Sam had become much more supportive, and they became receptive to his input.

During this stage of orienting players to new points of view, you will want to observe their commitment to learning. If they are open to new ideas and committed to learning how to increase their effectiveness, the probability of a successful coaching relationship will be very good.

Orienting is about sharing insight through two key steps:

1. Define and clarify the other person's current point of view in a way that enables the person to discover it is not effective.

2. Introduce an alternative perspective on the situation.

Accept: There are two dimensions to consider at the acceptance stage of coaching. First, the player will decide at this point whether or not to receive the new point of view that has been presented. That person alone must determine what to do with this information: consider it real, try to justify past behavior, discredit the source or just outright reject everything. You will observe the person's level of adaptability—just how open are they to new information and changing their approach. If the individual is open to the insights and objectives of other people, you will see a positive attitude and a willingness to listen, consider change and embrace different views. During this stage the Player-Coach can only listen, observe and provide clarification as needed. For lasting change to emerge, the individual being coached must demonstrate the willingness to make the necessary changes.

It is not uncommon for players to minimize feedback or problem areas after they've had time to process the information. This might become evident if they start rationalizing and giving you, the coach, a series of "yeah, buts". When this happens, remind them of the consequences of not learning from the information and how it might limit their future performance or personal ambitions.

Second, every Player-Coach must accept the decision made by the person they are coaching. If you have not struck motive in the person with the information you've shared, there will be no change in behavior. Accept their decision and save yourself heartburn and frustration. You cannot put the desire to change or to do things in a different way into a person. If the person does not demonstrate a willingness to make changes to be more effective, you probably have the wrong person on your team. The person who persists in being defensive and resistant to feedback may be a poor candidate for coaching.

On the other hand, those who accept the information, and demonstrate at least a moderately high willingness to understand how they can become more effective, are candidates for additional coaching and investment. The next challenge for them will be the degree to which they are able to make the required changes and sustain them. This will take intentional and measured actions over time, with regular coaching and adjustments along the way.

Accepting a new point of view requires:

1. Readiness of the person being coached to accept change.

2. The Player-Coach's acceptance of the decision made by the individual being coached.

Connect: The magic to achieving high morale in your people is in your ability to connect your corporate objectives to their personal interests and ambition. And when it is done successfully, the players reach deep within and contribute a level of talent and energy that you could never buy. This is what is called tapping into discretionary talent.

Part of the role of the Player-Coach is to challenge players to identify the areas where they can be more effective, and to set measurable objectives for improvement. And improvement, change and goal attainment come from focus—from concentration. Nothing happens without will power and desire harnessed to clearly defined goals. Once a person decides to accept and apply the new information the coach has presented, that person must focus energy on specific targets. The Player-Coach connects the people and the objectives, helping players use their talents in a way that benefits both the individuals and the group.

The ability to focus on an objective distinguishes high achievers from average performers. One of my mentors drilled into my head the importance of focus, and I have tried to employ the power of concentration—of seeing clearly and intently—throughout my professional life. This power creates the drive to overcome procrastination and over-thinking. People with powers of concentration are able to bring heroic energy to whatever they attempt. When members of a group can also collaborate, using their powers of concentration for a common goal, they can achieve limitless results.

The Player-Coach must know the players and their roles as well as a winning football quarterback understands all the positions on the team. The Player-Coach leverages the efforts of others by helping them understand where they fit into a larger pattern—how their own objectives are connected to common goals. This allows players to turn their powers of concentration on those goals without feeling they are abandoning their own personal objectives.

In the classic speech "The Strangest Secret," Earl Nightingale, renowned self-improvement author and founder of Nightingale-Conant, says, "If you only care enough for a result you will almost certainly attain it." A Player-Coach helps others feel that it's not only safe but imperative to "care enough."

Connecting is:

1. Understanding how personal and group objectives are meshed.

2. Linking and leveraging the will of the players and the Player Coach.

3. Employing the powers of concentration—seeing what needs to be done clearly and intently—and collaboration.

4. Setting meaningful and measurable goals.

Hope: Hope is intrinsic to being alive and to what it means to live a fulfilling life. For centuries, philosophers and theologians have considered hope a universal human search. What would life be without the promise of a future? We are creatures who find great sense of purpose in creating that future.

When we coach other people, our aim must be to help them envision, seize, embrace and shape their future. Showing them what is possible and how to attain it gives hope for the big win, the reward.

Retaining top talent will be determined by the degree to which those players believe they have a future with you and your organization. Nothing drains young talent of ambition and commitment more thoroughly than the realization that opportunities for advancement are limited or nonexistent. The best will expect great opportunity and the hope that opportunity embodies.

Hope is showing the way to the win and to all the rewards it holds for those who are strong enough to attain it.

Hope is holding forth a vision for what is possible in the bright tomorrow. Where people lack vision, there is no desire to concentrate on tomorrow.

Hope inspires ordinary people to accomplish extraordinary results. Learn the art of coaching hope in your people and you will be amazed at the return on your investment.

Hope requires you to:

1. Believe the best of yourself and others.

2. Be forward-thinking and -acting in the development of talented people.

3. Show the way by expecting the desired outcomes will be attained.

4. Lift people out of mediocrity by calling on them to give that part of themselves you can never buy. It is the level of commitment and ability that emerges out of their soul, for which the highest and only reward is a deep sense of personal satisfaction, pride and self-worth. It may be driven by a desire to be the best or the fear of being second-best. It may even be driven by anger or the need to prove someone wrong. Whatever the motive, never cheapen that effort with a monetary reward. Only the win will do.

Get the best from your leaders. Give the best of you!

EXECUTE THE PLAYER-COACH APPROACH WITH YOUR TEAM!

SCHEDULE A PLAYER-COACH LEADER SEMINAR

What participants will gain:

- Learn the 4 stages of Player-Coach leadership
- COACH model — 5 levels of engagement
- Leverage and dimensions of adaptability
- Coaching assessments
- Practical steps for implementing the Player-Coach approach
- How to leverage yourself through the talent of others

Schedules:

- Half day session (4 hours) or Full day (7 hours)

**For more information go to: Playercoachleader.com
Or, call Lamar Hamilton at 952-829-0651**

HERE'S HOW TO ORDER MORE BOOKS!

Book offer and details

To order more copies of, *Player-Coach Leader, Leverage the Talent Around You* simply go to www.playercoachleader.com.

Books are just $14.95 each and with orders of 10 or more books you will receive a discount of $2.00 off each book for a price of $12.95 each!

Shipping and handling is extra. Please expect 7-10 days for delivery in the U.S. See web site for more information.

NOTES

NOTES

NOTES

NOTES

_____

_____

_____

_____

_____

_____

_____

_____

_____

_____

_____